The Spaces Between

The Spaces Between

KAILA-TRISH MASA

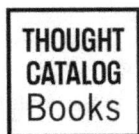

THOUGHT CATALOG Books

BROOKLYN, NY

THOUGHT
CATALOG
Books

Collective
World

Cover designed by Althier Alianza.

Published by Thought Catalog Books, a publishing house owned by The Thought & Expression Co., Williamsburg, Brooklyn.

Second edition, 2017

ISBN: 978-1945796722

Printed and bound in the United States.

10 9 8 7 6 5 4 3 2 1

CONTENTS

Prologue

Hopefully someday
I'll have the
Courage
To tell you
That you made
Me this way
That you are the
One I wrote for
And every single thing
I wrote is
About you,
Only you

I

To Crave

There's always that one thing
that one thing you'd always crave
crave to touch
crave to feel
crave to do.
For me, it's you.
No matter how much I try to pull away
I just can't
I will always come back.
Again and
Again.

Shooting Stars

Stars fall
Through the sky
Too fast
Too unpredictable
Like how I fell
For you
So fast
So unpredictable
Again and
Again.

Aberrant

Can you feel my heart beating?
Can you feel it thumping against my chest
Like rain pelting on the roof?
This is me
Me and my heart
With its aberrant pulse
Loving you
Loving you with all of me

At Night

You're the sunshine
To my shadowed soul
The missing piece
To make me whole

Every moment you breathe
You give me life
Like how the sun gives
Light to the moon at night

It

Closed eyes
Steady breaths
Fingers entwined
Warm embraces

A dream I don't want
To wake up from
A path I'll take
Leading home

You're it for me
Darling, you are
You're all I see
Even from afar

Translucence

Sometimes I wish I know how your mind works
To know what you're thinking
To know if I ever cross your mind
Sometimes I wish to hear the words you say
To hear you say amazing things
To hear you say my name
But more often than not,
I wish to see you
To see how you look at things,
To see how you look at me
And if you'd have that certain twinkle in your eyes
That would tell me you're happy that you do
Sometimes, or more oftentimes,
I do

Lost In You

I'd like to believe that the words you say
And the words you write
Are for me
The same way that mine are for you
But most of all,
I'd like to think that you're thinking about me too
That every single thought running through your head
Is about me
The way all thoughts racing
Through mine
Are about you

Euphony

I hold onto you
Like a melody
Of my favourite song
I keep on singing
I'm gasping for air
I'm breathing you in
In ways I couldn't comprehend

Flickering Light

You were a candle brightly lit
In a room so dark
I was nothing but a moth
Drawn to your light flickering
I got too close
Too close that I got burned
But,
What if things were different
Where tables were turned
Would you be like me
Consumed and burnt?

Secrets

She writes
Pours herself
Hoping that somehow
You'd realize
It is you
You who filled her head
With impossibilities
You who she's writing about
You who she's writing for

Maze

Don't get lost in the maze my mind made,
Like I did
Don't lose yourself in the mess inside me,
The way I still am

II

Fall

She was Fall
She faded away
With the falling of snow
On cracked pavements
She slipped away,
Silent goodbye whispered to
Shadows of the autumn sun
Her promise of tomorrow
Resonates through
The broken windows
Of an empty house

No Regrets

Loving until there's nothing left
Loving whole, nonetheless
Loving to the point of death
Falling deeply
Falling true
Falling with no regrets

Perennial

Some goodbyes
They're meant forever
Some others
Only for a time
We really couldn't tell
But darling
The way you held me in your arms
I know
It wouldn't be the last
I swear

Onwards

We have to move on
Whether we like to or not
Whether we're prepared
It's not a matter of wanting or waiting
But a matter of needing
Because life goes on
Life won't wait

Infinite

This is me
Someone more
Than I was yesterday
Infinitely less of
The person I could be
Tomorrow

In Time

You said the words I needed to hear
Now my heart soars
And my doubt disappears
I know I could do more
I'll get better at it
You just wait and see
I'll be the best I can be

III

Hurricane

Wisps of eerie silence
Hang on the stale
Shadow of loneliness
As bright sunlight
Dimmed the blinding
Thirst for a single drop
Of your melancholic rain
Oh but you are
A beauty
A beauty of raging storms
And torrential rains,
Of violent waves and dark clouds
You are a beauty
Terrible and
Beautiful

Decadent

You are my own little piece of heaven

Beneath It All

I get lost in the beauty of everything I see

Drunk

I am drunk on the beauty of something I cannot have

One-Liner

I can't seem to find the words to say to you

Blurred

I can't understand you

Bed Weather

It's cold and I need your arms around me

Inescapable

I yearn for your touch,
the way the ocean yearns for the shore

When I Look Into Your Eyes

All I see is the reflection of a girl pretending
she's different from who she used to be

I Am Yours

I am yours
I am lost in you
Lost in your lingering gazes,
In your fleeting touches
You pierce through
My lungs,
Leaving me gasping
For air
Every time
You are near
I crave for you
You are my addiction
The kind I wouldn't want to get over
I could drown in you
And never would I want
To be saved
I long to get lost
In your thoughts
The way I lost myself
In mine

I am lost
I am lost in you
And I don't want to be found
Because I want you,
I want to be with you
Even if it means
Losing myself
In finding you

Dearest

I knew from the moment my eyes met yours
That my heart will always
Belong to you
That your touch will
Forever be imprinted
On the surface of my inked hands
And that our memories will
Remain tattooed on my mind
Because every day that pass,
My heart sings only of your name
Again and again
And I'll tell you this
Over and over
So you wouldn't forget
Until the sun stops rising
And the moon stops shining,
Until the world stops revolving
And until the day after forever,
My heart is yours, love

IV

Winter

She was Winter
Her shaded heart
Blazed incandescently
In the darkness
Of the night
And the arms of dawn
Cradled her aching soul
With the warmth of
The rising sun
As her misted eyes
Held the silhouette of the
Yesterday
She dreamt about

Break Me

Break me apart,
Pick my broken pieces
And piece me back together
Love my parts
And love me whole
It's how things start
From nothing
To little,
To much bigger
And so much more

Scars

Scars do not
Make you
Any less of who
You are;
They don't define
You

Saving Grace

Sometimes I think I don't deserve you
You are too much
Too much for my measly soul
Too much for my broken heart
Too much for my shattered dreams
But here you are
Never giving up on me,
Even when I myself want to
You complete me
You mend my broken heart
You pick up the pieces of my shattered dreams
You are the light to my darkness
The ray of hope in my despair
The love in all of my pain
You save me
More than you could ever know

Forget-me-not

Somehow she believes that she's lost and wandering
Trying to find meaning in what she does
Trying to make sense of what she believes in
But she always wondered if everything she did
Amounted to something
Or anything at all.
That's what she fears most
That when the time comes and life ends,
Will people remember her?

What It Meant

She got used to keeping everything to herself
Wallowing,
Drowning in her misery
How she loved when you came to her rescue
When you can tell she's putting up a façade
Faking a smile
Because you see her
You know her
Intimately and thoroughly,
From the way the corner of her eyes crinkle
When she laughs
Or how her eyebrows furrow when she's mad
To the way her mood abruptly shifts for no reason
Or how her voice quivers when she's about to cry
Everything matters to her
She realized that she's not invisible
That she's not forgotten
That it was possible for someone to care for her
That she mattered

V

To Spring

Remnants of my
Withering self
Settled on worn
Asphalt pavements
Swimming in colors
Of goodbye
And the welcoming breeze
Embraced frail bodies
In symphonies of
Warm hues and
Dried foliage
I faded away
My present
Drifted
Into your future

Lost

I was holding your hand I was sure of that
You were gone the instant I closed my eyes
We kept pacing back and forth,
Back and forth
Now I don't know where to go anymore

Parallel

We live in parallel universes
Always alongside
But never congruent
We trudge similar paths
But never do we
Find ourselves meeting
At some point

Until This Day

Things didn't turn out the way I wanted it to
Now we're both so indifferent to even bother to
Patch things up and make everything okay
Something we've always been until this day

I Wish

I wish I could
Make everything
Fade
Make everything
Go away
I wish I could
Hold you
In my arms
Hold you
Until your heart stops beating
Forever,
I wish I could
Have you forever
But I think it's
Too much
To ask

VI

Untitled I

Hand poised in the air
You were ready to write on me,
To imprint your story on the gritty surface
Of my skin
Because that's what I am to you
That's what I am meant to be – a slate
Impermanence mars my skin,
Temporary words and passing thoughts
Fill the spaces of my roughened exterior
My existence screams of possibilities
And endless outlines of a future
You crave for
And dust from my past settles on the
Wooden edges of my face
You define me,
You know who I am,
What I am

But who am I really,
How will I know
When all I've ever done was
Feel every word you write,
Catch the dust of your mistakes and
Allow you to change them,
How do I define myself
When all I've ever been was a
Means for your end

Under The Waves

Under the waves,
Lie my wandering
Little soul
Caught in a riptide of
Hellos
And goodbyes
Like the sequences
Of dancing city lights
Oh I am under the waves
Under the
Mesmerizing beauty of
Short-lived loved affairs
Swallowed by the
Promise of the
Setting sun
On the surface of
The rolling tidal
Waves

Disappear

As easy as it came
It slipped from my fingertips
Gone in an instant
Gone with the wind

Ad Interim

It was temporary
A taste of something so sweet
Yet it disappeared so suddenly
Leaving nothing
But that bittersweet taste
Of defeated victory

Silhouette

Your eyes are telling me
What your mouth couldn't
They speak of memories
We've long cherished
I saw myself in them
A silhouetted dream
Now,
Your eyes no longer speak

Inconstant

I was blinded by your light
Caught unaware, caught unprepared
And then suddenly it was dark again
You let yourself shine someplace else

Dreaming

Before,
my nights were filled by you
by your words
by your stories
by your humor
Now,
my nights are filled with dreams of you
dreams of having you
dreams of me and you

Losing Forever

We lose some
And gain some
I lost you
But you lost me too
We both thought
Leaving would mean
Gaining more
It's sad to say though
We lost ourselves,
We lost our hearts
And we lost what we had, forever

Beauty

You've always told me
I have eyes
That could see the beauty
In everything
And now I wonder if
The beauty I saw
In you
Was real
Because all those times,
I believed everything
Was beautiful because
You were there
You were there to put stars in my eyes
You,
Were the one to put beauty
In me
And now that you're gone,
Nothing makes
Sense anymore

Irreparable

How can you repair something so broken? Like glass shattered into million tiny pieces, powdered to dust like my heart, when you went and left and never looked back.

VII

Quilted

The dark, silken sky
Cradled the moon and the stars
And embraced them
With the gentleness
Of the cold, midnight breeze
As delicate fingers traced
The silhouettes of
Broken lines and lost conversations,
Sounds of heavy footsteps and
Soft stuttering breaths
Echo in the unlit
Hallways of empty, quiet houses
And whispers of the past
Are ghosts hiding behind
Closed doors,
Living,

Breathing,
Feeding on the silence
Infinitely surrounding
Fragmented words
Written on loose sheets
Tucked under old,
Stained quilts

The End

How could I even close my eyes?
When I do, it's the only thing I see
Your face when I told you about me
I couldn't take it, so I turned and left
'Cause what I saw was what I was afraid of,
What I saw was
The end

Unarmored

You held my heart
On the palm of your
Cold, clammy hands
And all the while I thought
You were the armor
That'd protected my
Wandering, little soul
Oh how wrong I was
To think you'd shield me from pain
To think you'd chase
Bullets to save me.
You weren't my armor;
You were the pain
The bullet that shot
My heart into spirals
Of misery and loss
You weren't my armor;
You were my destruction

Laughter

She laughed
Not with you
Nor at you
But at herself
For believing it could be
Something more

Knee-Deep

Thoughts of you
Consumed every part
Of my being
Memories of us
Tainted my blood
With the bitter taste of
Heartbreak
And my heart's been marked
With intricate tattoos of our
Short-lived love affair
I miss you
I really do
And every day that pass
Without you in my arms
Is like drowning in
Knee deep water
I claw my way out
To the surface
And try to push
Warm, salty air
Through my constricted lungs
'I miss you' and
'I love you'
Pass through my cracked lips
In dire need of yours
I miss you,
I love you

I really do
And my plea for you
To come back
Is lost with the
Setting of the sun on the
Horizon

Untangle

Your smell,
Your touch,
Your gaze
They all linger
Even through the
Deepest corners
Of the deepest
Parts of my heart
The parts I thought couldn't be reached
The parts I didn't know existed
But here you are
Living,
Breathing
And searing yourself
Inside of me
How I wish
To untangle myself
From every thought
Of you

Whispers & Musings

Sometimes she stops and asks,

"Are you thinking about me too?"

Numb

And now as I stare at you,
I have this gaping hole inside me
But somehow I feel like it was a long time ago
Since I held my heart open for you
That it doesn't hurt me anymore

VIII

Untitled II

I am a puzzle you cannot solve
A jumbled mess
Of random,
Uneven pieces of
You,
Disproportionately
Dusting my skin
With thoughts and
Memories that
Cloud your mind
Your dainty fingers
Etch colorful words
On the tainted
Shell of my soul
And every delicate brush
Of your fingertips
Leaves parts of you

On me
And I on you
I held onto your
Brokenness,
The way the sky
Embraced the stars
In its vastness
I kept your parts
But
You didn't keep mine
Day by day,
You come and go
And each time
You take a fraction of my whole
Leaving only gaps
To fill the missing pieces
You stole

Definitely, Maybe

Torn between wanting and not wanting to know
Torn between wanting and not wanting to ask
Maybe that's just the way it goes,
Maybe that's how it is
More often than not,
We're too eager to know the answers
But too afraid to ask the questions

Circles & Squares

You're a circle,
I'm a square
The more I try to fit
The more it hurts
Smoothing my edges
To fit your curves
Always ends
With me nursing
My wounded self

Stay

Stay with me please,
I'm begging you
I'm too scared to trudge this road alone
Please, my dear
Hold my hand and never disappear

IX

Trespass

I let you in,
I let you inside my world
I was amazed at how you become an
Unwavering presence in my life
How you slowly embedded yourself
In my little spaces
How you opened yourself
For me to get to know more
But I was too far gone when I realized
The thing I thought was real and permanent
Was just a figment of my imagination
I should've known things will change,
They always do
I should've known you didn't see and feel the way I do
I should've kept myself distant,
I should've

Now, I'm left hanging
Left with nothing but memories,
Memories I'm struggling to preserve
Because as you turned around, I did nothing
But stare at your retreating back
And hope that you'll turn and come back again

On The Edge

I'm holding on a tightrope
Trying to pull you in
But you lose your hold
And you let go
Though I keep pulling
Hoping deep within
You'd reach out and pull me too
In that time then,
I'd let you

Yet Again

You're always that
And you'll always be —
The exception for her
No matter how much she promises that she won't
No matter how much she does not hope to
She would always talk to you
She would be the first to start the conversation
She would make up reasons why she should
Break her promises
Just for you

Sadly, you can't do the same
She isn't an exception for you
She is nothing
No one
So you just push her away
And set her aside
But she does not care
She keeps on picking up pieces of herself

And tries to put them back together
She always does
Every
Single
Day

You & I

Oftentimes, my head is filled
With endless thoughts
Of you
Of the possibilities we could've had
The possibilities of You and I,
Of Us,
Now,
Even with my constant denial,
I still hope and long
For that tiny spark of possibility
For that single moment when your eyes
Twinkle when you say,
'I love you too'
And please, when the time comes that you
Realize that you do,
You know where to find me
I'll be there
Waiting for you

Give Me One Good Reason

Make me stay,
Give me one good reason
Why I shouldn't forget,
One good reason why
I shouldn't let the memories
Be swept away
Make me stay,
Give me one good reason
Why I should leave my heart
On the palm of
Your calloused hands
Make me stay,
Please, darling,
Make me stay

Nocturnal

Midnights,
The time
My words
Seem to come to
Life
Undeniably
The time
When my mind
Pours
And my heart
Breaks

Nostalgia

I miss you but you seem better off without me
I miss you then I miss you some more
I miss you but it doesn't matter anymore
Everything changed
From what was once to what was then

Happy Thoughts

"Happy thoughts,
Think of happy thoughts"
That's what you always say
But my happy thoughts have been and will always be
Filled by thoughts of you and me

X

Darling

Who broke your fragile,
Little heart,
Darling?
Who broke you
And
Let you
Bleed poetry on
Torn, crumpled pieces of paper?

Would You

When I tell you I'm feeling sad,
Would you make me smile?
When I tell you I'm feeling down,
Would you lift me up?
When I tell you I'm nowhere near okay,
Would you go to the ends of the earth to save me?

Depletion

From a thousand words
It narrowed down to one
Now I'm lucky
If I could have one

Fear

She fears more
But sees much differently
Somehow the things she fears before
Evolved into something her heart can't grasp so easily

Divergence

It's sad when people you're close to slowly drift away, leaving behind only memories, faded and cloudy. It's like they're moving forward when you're still stuck to the time when everything was fine, when everything was going great, when you were happy. It hurts a lot when people you consider a part of your life become people you just once knew. But nothing in this world is permanent. People come and go, explained and unexplained, slowly then suddenly. In the end, you're left with nothing and no one but yourself and your memories. You keep to yourself all the longing and hope that somewhere, in the deepest creases of their mind, they think about you and that a piece of their heart misses you the way you miss them.

XI

Spring

He was Spring
He awoke to the
Singing of trees and
Billowing leaves
His eyes opened
To the brilliance
Of phantasmagoric
Lights
Pirouetting in
Whirlpools of
Murky puddles
As tremors of
The Earth's jovial
Laughter
Tingled on
The surface of his
Moistened skin

Wonder

I want to have eyes that always
see the wonder in everything

Daydreaming

I once said it was nothing
To be honest,
It was everything
The way you touched my hair
The way you whispered in my ear
I get tingles
I feel giddy
But at the back
Of my mind
I keep thinking
Am I daydreaming?

Destiny

Here I am
There you are
I'm a lost soul
So are you
We brushed past each other
Started on
Our happily ever after

Gypsy

I was a wanderer
A traveller
And my heart—a desert
Was parched and
Shrivelled
Then I found you
(Or maybe you found me)
And finding you was like
Finding an oasis,
So full of life
Suddenly,
All too quickly
I was drunk
Drunk on you
Drunk on the love
You so graciously
Offered
And now,
I am no longer
A wanderer
I found my home
In you
And my heart—no longer a desert
Is quenched and
Submerged

Sunset

Intertwined
Underneath that velvet
Sunset sky
The sun bids goodbye
But I know, my love
It will take forever
To loosen
The knot
That binds us
Together

XII

Untitled III

Back and forth,
Parts of you
Tumble against me,
Passing in
Tangent arrays of
Multicolored debris
But
I will not let
Them stay
I will not let
Them linger on
My chapped skin,
I will not let
Them define me
For
I am my own

When Summer Is Gone

Cold, brittle breeze
Dissipates on the cracks
Of fallen autumn foliage
As the winking sun
Flickers its golden light
And embraces
The crisp mornings
In its welcoming haze

Lay Me Gently

You were like rain
Pelting on the sun-kissed
Surface of my skin
Your soft-breathing
Seeps through
The cracks of my
Sleeping bones
As your melodic murmurs
Lay me gently
In the cradle
Of your warm,
Rumpled sheets

Autumn Is More Than

She is Autumn
And she is more than
Her brokenness,
More than the
Evanescent warmth
In her erratically beating
Heart
She is Fall
And she leaves
Parts of herself
Intertwined
On cracked pavements
In trails of
Colorful goodbyes

Mismatched

She was a constellation
Of mismatched pieces,
Her eyes held
Flickers of fairy tales and
Happily ever afters
But,
Her hands
Bled harsh truths and
Broken-hearted goodbyes

Devoid

I'm losing,
Losing
Losing
A part of
Myself
Everyday,
Every
Single
Day
And I fear
The day when
Nothing will
Be left of
Me

Left-over

Perhaps,
What's left of me
Are those
Unwanted parts,
Parts no one
Desired,
Parts too wrecked
To be salvaged
Maybe that's
Why no one
Ever stayed

A Brilliant Mess

You are here,
Your heart's been
Beaten,
Pounded and
Broken
Far too many times
But you are still here, darling
You are
Still here
And that means
So much

XIII

Psychedelic

The sky bursts
With infinities of kaleidoscopic lights
Dancing
To the music
Of erratically beating
Hearts
Intertwined in
Webs of quiet
Lullabies and
Soft-spoken poetry
As glitters of sunlight
Blanketed
The sultry waves
Of the ocean

Invasion

Come to me, darling
Invade my eternity
Oh, invade my soul!

For Every

I look at you
And all I see is
A beautiful person
A person so broken
Yet so perfectly imperfect,
When I look at your scars,
It's not the flaws I see,
Not the bumps and jagged marks,
But the strength and courage behind them
And I love you for it
For every broken piece
For every jagged scar
For every imperfection
I love you,
I really do

Savior

You always seem to know the
Right words to say
The words I badly needed to hear
Even before
I realize that
I needed to hear them
And I thank you for it
Because you don't know
How many times you've saved
My heart from breaking into
Millions of pieces
And how you've saved my soul
From drowning

Good In You

There is good in you
As there is within me
No amount of heartbreaks
And pain
No number of flaws and
Mistakes
Can change that

Heartbreaks

My heart belongs to heartbreaks
My hands bleed to write about pain
And loss and misery
I'm a mouthful of almosts and could've beens
And I spend every day trying to
Find the perfect words,
The perfect set of words that could describe
Every broken piece of me

Jar Of Happiness

Seeing you is like opening my own personal jar of happiness. Your smile could light up a room, even the darkest. It's not just your smile, to be honest. It's you, it is in you. It is as if you were born to light up the world and you were born to share your happiness with every single one of us. And I am happy, not just because you are, but because I have come to know you. I have come to know such a genuine and beautiful soul and it makes me believe that there is beauty in everything, there is hope in every minute and there is love in everyone.

XIV

Summer

I am Summer
My heart no longer new
Fire burns
Through my
Velvet veins
And
Vibrant hues
Gleam beneath my
Windowed soul
As fluorescent sparks
Ignite
Spectrums of
My entirety

To Feel Alive

'Cause that's what scars do to you
You spend minutes, even hours in a day
Thinking that at any moment
Your scars would re-open again
And swallow you whole,
Bathe you in blood of pain and loss
And leave you gasping for air
Through your pierced, deflated lungs
That's what scars do to you,
They make you expect
Wounds and pain
And you prepare yourself
For it
You wait for it
But it never comes
And maybe a little part of yourself
Is disappointed
Because at times,
You crave pain
You crave feeling something other than
Numbness
Something other than 'okay'
Feeling pain made you feel
Alive

Demons

Each one of us has our own demons
Inside our closets,
Under our beds
As for mine,
It lives
And breathes
And grows
Inside my head

Good Kind Of Sad

Many thought sadness was a mess of tear-stained faces and red-rimmed eyes, eyes looking bleak and empty and lost. Many thought sadness was the result of losing someone, of losing something, of being nothing and no one. But the real kind of sadness, the gut-wrenching, heart-breaking kind of sadness, is the sadness hidden beneath brittle smiles and weary eyes, eyes trying to hide the truth, smiles trying to convince other people of a make-believe happiness. It is the kind of sadness that leaves you breathless, not the good kind, but the kind that leaves you desperately trying to catch your breath, desperately trying to fill your lungs with air, desperately trying to fill yourself with life. And this is the kind of sadness that's inevitable. The kind that catches you unaware, unprepared. It is the sadness that lasts a lifetime, no matter what how many people you have in your life, no matter who you are or who you've become. But learn to love it. Learn to live with it. Embrace it. And maybe someday, this sadness, this sadness that breaks your heart, this sadness that's inevitable, will leave you breathless, not the bad kind, but the good kind this time.

Acquaintance

You told me that in time, I'd forget the pain. That the pain will go away. But then I realized that no, the pain doesn't go away. It just sinks through the crevices and corners of our bodies until the time comes that we get used to it. The pain doesn't go away, we just acquaint with it. Perhaps, that's what I did; I became my pain's acquaintance. And somehow along the way, I fell in love with it.

XV

Epilogue

I fear that one day,
When I wake up
All of my memories of you,
Of you and I,
Will be erased, will be forgotten
So I spend my time writing,
Pouring my heart out
On loose pages of a notebook
Tattooing my memories in black ink
And if one day,
When the time comes
That I could no longer remember,
Or that you couldn't anymore,
Somehow, people would know our story
Of how we met,
Of how we fell in love
And of how our hearts were broken

Without You Knowing

You,
You let me bleed
Endlessly
On crisp white papers
You left me,
You left me to bleed
Endlessly
And
You didn't
Even know
That you
Did

Mirror

Am I as
Broken
As you are
And
Are you as
Broken
As I am?

Frenetic

Hands in frenetic
Tangle of endless
Possibilities
Of futures
That have yet
To unfold,
You
And I
With a mouthful of words,
Unsaid and
Unspoken
'I love you'
Dancing on the
Tips of our tongues
Waiting for the music
To start

Untold

We weren't anything
To one another
We were nothing,
We were
Just two people
Who (may have)
Loved one another
But didn't have
The courage to
Say it

If Only

If only I could hear your thoughts
If only I could read them,
It could have saved me from a whole lot of
Heartaches
I could've protected my heart
Because then I would know when
You'd be saying
'I'm not in love with you.
I never was.'

Three Words

It took me a thousand words
To break through your walls
And maybe, even more, to forget about you.
But it only took you three words
To break through mine
And only one to break me.

Eternal

My heart takes more than a second to slow down,
More than a minute to settle and
More than forever to get over you

Still Am, Will Always Be

I am yours
But
Maybe you aren't mine

I am yours
Though your heart
Says otherwise

I am yours
Even if I know
You are
Not mine
And
Will never be

Almost Always

We let go of people
And things,
We set them free
Hoping they would
Come back.
Sadly,
Almost always,
They don't.

Could Have Been

Once upon a time
You were mine
And I was yours
But,
Love became
Too much
For us to handle
Now,
We were nothing
But a fairy tale
That almost happened

All At Once

I'd rather lose you,
Lose all of you
All at once
Than feel you slowly,
Slowly drifting
Away from me

Nothing But Lost

I lost you
Slowly,
Piece by piece
We drifted apart,
Losing
And losing
Until we're
Nothing but
Lost

I Only Almost Did

I wanted you to be mine
I longed for you to be mine,
All the while I thought
I had you,
But the things is,
I never did have you
I only
Almost did

Open-Ended

I am not good with goodbyes
I never was
So when you left
I never did get the chance
To tell you

Sad Love

Sometimes I wonder if I really did fall in love with you, if I really did give my heart to you. Because as time pass and as my heart continues to beat, I am thinking that maybe I just fell in love with the idea of you, fell in love with the idea of someone falling for me, fell in love with the idea of falling in love.

No More

Yes,
I missed you and
Maybe I still do.
But my heart,
My heart finally
Learned how to
Silently miss you,
How to miss you less,
To miss you with
No more heartaches,
No more tear-stained pillowcases,
No more cries of longing
And desperation.
Yes, I still miss you and
Probably, I'll always will
But my heart,
My heart no longer breaks
Every time I miss you

Thank You

To my ever-loving parents: thank you for always believing in me, for always pushing me to strive harder and be a better person, for never failing to support me in achieving all of my dreams. No words can express how grateful I am for having you in my life. I love you very much! This is for you.

To my sisters: thank you for always supporting me, for putting up with all my (occasional) lapses, especially when I'm writing, for (sometimes) laughing at my lame jokes and for letting me bear-hug and kiss you every time I want to. I love you both to bits!

To Althier: thank you for creating such a wonderful book cover, for making it the way I had envisioned it to be. I will always be a fan of your art, Ching.

To all my friends (who may or may not be buying this out of obligation): thank you for always being there for me, for always listening to all my rants and raves about anything and everything, for being so appreciative, for relating to the things that I write and never failing to tell me so.

To Sir Oliver: thank you for helping me make all of this possible, for helping me become a better writer, for making me love poetry more. Thank you for always listening and understanding the poet in me.

To you: thank you for letting my words occupy a space in your heart, for reading and connecting with my poetry, for loving them enough to keep them permanently in your hands. Thank you for being a home to this little one.

Most especially to God: thank You for giving me words, for the ability to make something out of them, for the passion to share and inspire others, for the second life you so graciously gifted me. All glory goes to You!

About the Author

Kaila-Trish Masa is a writer from the Philippines. Her works have been featured in Thought Catalog and Berlin ArtParasites.

Tumblr: beneathunspokenwords.tumblr.com
Instagram: beneathunspokenwords

www.ingramcontent.com/pod-product-compliance
Lightning Source LLC
Chambersburg PA
CBHW031623040426
42452CB00007B/638